This book belongs to

_____

Ninja Life Hacks™

This book is dedicated to my children - Mikey, Kobe, and Jojo.

On the fifth question of the test, Smart Ninja came upon a problem he'd never seen before.

Many ninjas would have given up at this point, but not Smart Ninja.
He knew that if he gave his best effort, he would eventually succeed.
He had learned to focus on his effort more than his intelligence.

Smart Ninja didn't always possess a growth mindset.

He once thought that *intelligence* and *talent* were the determining factors of success. This is called a fixed mindset.

In contrast, when you hold a growth mindset you believe that effort and hard work determine your success.

For example, Smart Ninja was great at many things but he would avoid anything he wasn't naturally good at.

He excelled at all subjects in school. But when work didn't come easy to him, he would complain...

When he started a new hobby and he didn't pick it up right away, he would get discouraged.

He would believe that he didn't have enough skill or talent to succeed.

His whole world opened up when Patient Ninja introduced him to a concept that would change his mindset forever.

While working on a project one day, Smart Ninja became frustrated that he couldn't figure something out quickly.

It took Smart Ninja several tries, but he finally got it.

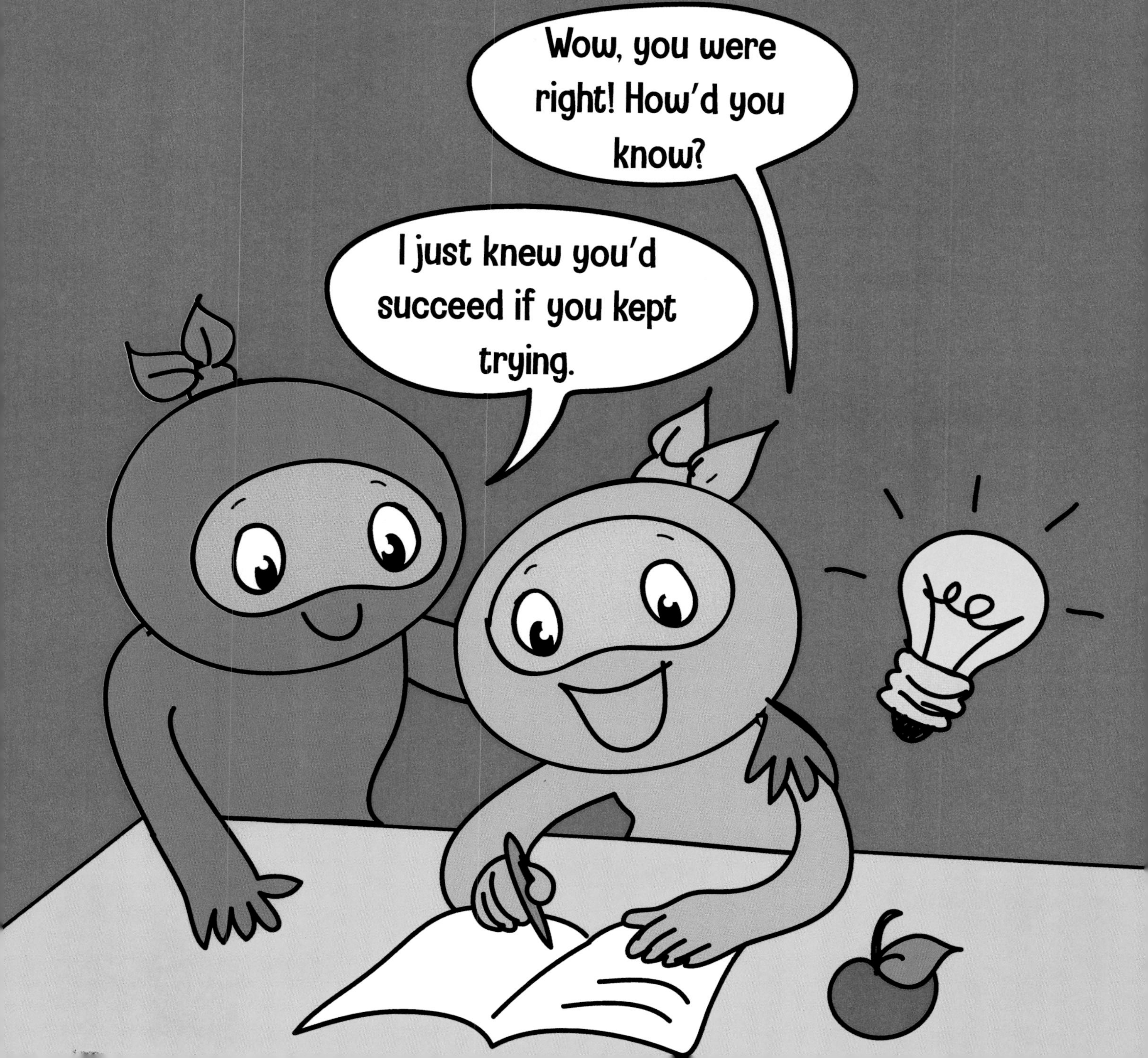

"It's a strategy I use called the E.O.I. strategy. It stands for Effort Over Intelligence. It means with anything I do, I believe I can become successful as long as I keep trying," explained Patient Ninja.

"There will be some things in life that will come easily to me, but other things will not come so easily. So the most important characteristic that will serve me the most is effort."

Smart Ninja lay in bed that night thinking about what his friend had said.
He had always thought that being smart and talented determined everything.
But what his friend had said made so much sense.
As long as I keep trying, I can achieve anything.

He slowly began to adopt the E.O.I. strategy.

Soon, he had changed his fixed mindset into a growth mindset.

He began to look for opportunities to grow instead of hiding from them.

He was okay with failing as long as he was progressing
in whatever it was he was learning to do.

Smart Ninja focused more on effort and hard work instead of how smart or talented he was.

This made all the difference when he was presented with really hard things!

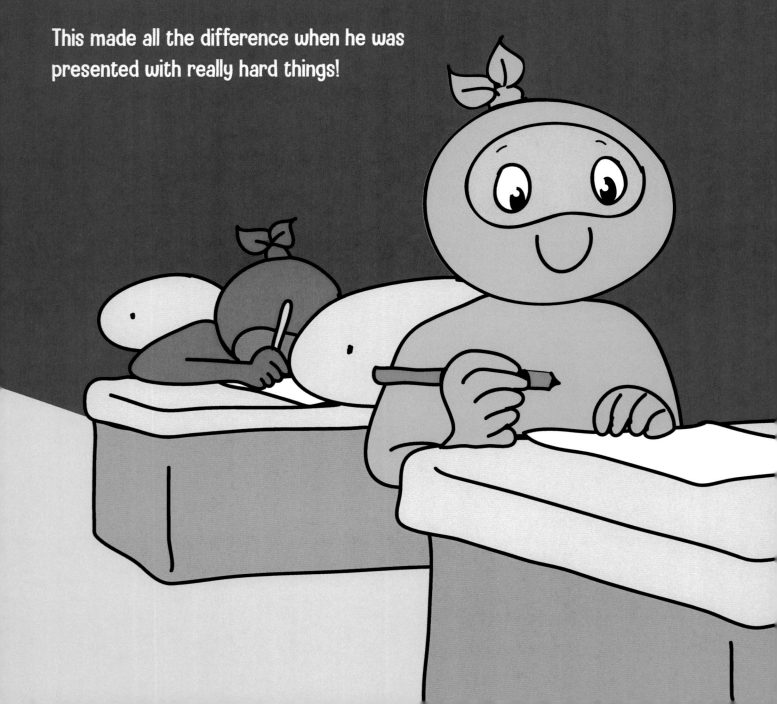

Your best weapon against a fear of failing could just be the E.O.I. concept!

Check out the Ninja Life Hacks box sets at ninjalifehacks.tv

 @marynhin   @GrowGrit
#NinjaLifeHacks

 Mary Nhin   Grow Grit

Grow Grit

Made in the USA
Las Vegas, NV
13 April 2021